The Waves Beneath My Feet

Amy Bastin

BookLeaf Publishing

India | USA | UK

Presentation by *BookLeaf Publishing*

Web: www.bookleafpub.com

E-mail: info@bookleafpub.com

ISBN: 978-93-5761-192-3

First edition 2022

DEDICATION

To the girl who fought to be here and never gave in to the pain - we did it.

ACKNOWLEDGEMENT

To Mum, Alex and Shaun,
Thank you always for your support and
encouragement.

PREFACE

These poems are inspired by the various waves
of emotion I have experienced in my life thus
far. A piece of my soul is printed on these pages.
Some of the poems are happy, some of them are
sad, but all of it is authentically me which is all I
ever wanted this collection to be.

Beth

Years ago on this day,
You took your final breath.
Twenty-seventh of June,
We lost you, Beth.

November was the month,
I first saw my mother cry.
I soon joined her,
When she explained why.

What started as an ache,
Soon became much more.
Little did you know,
Cancer had declared war.

You fought for seven months,
Six more than doctors thought.
Although in the harshest way,
A valuable lesson was taught.

Don't take life for granted,
With family, don't be slack.
You don't know what you have,
Until you can not get it back.

Live life to the fullest,
Don't let the evil in.
Never give up,
Life might throw you a win.

My heart still aches,
I still mourn your death.
I lost my second mother,
I miss you, Beth.

Little Girl

I was just a little girl
Innocent, hopeful, full of dreams
I was just a little girl
Whose soul was filled with screams

I was just a young girl
Confused, broken, mourning
I was just a young girl
When the darkness came calling

I was just a teenage girl
Lost, alone, terrified
I was just a teenage girl
When the thoughts left me paralysed

I was just a young woman
Cautious, sceptical, untrusting
I was just a young woman
Who found the world confronting

I am now a woman
Hurting, trying, healing
I am now a woman
Breaking free from the dark feeling

Depression

Your smile seems brighter, like sunshine on a
cloudy day
But your eyes don't shine like they used to
I can see the pain swimming in the windows to
your soul
And I know your world is dark

Once you would dance when the music played
Now you hardly register the sound
The things that would once have you enthralled
for hours
Now they bring no joy

The thoughts are impossible to drown out
But you don't want anyone to worry
Every day, every minute, every breath is a battle
Tomorrow doesn't feel like a reward

Some moments feel empty, cold or numb
Others are a searing pain
But unless someone else had felt that pain
They can never understand

It's dark and alone in the never-ending black
All light seemingly lost

But for as long as there is a heartbeat and air in
your lungs
I beg you to fight

Fight for the happiness you remember keeping
you warm
It is not gone, just lost
You don't have to be the pain this world has
caused
It doesn't have to be permanent

You are stronger than you think and feel
That's why you're still here
You are so much more than the darkness
drowning you
This doesn't have to be the end

How can I know how this pain suffocates?
How can I have hope?
Because I have been in the painful darkness
And I'm still here

First Love

I needed you to hurt me
And feed into my fears
I needed you to break me
And cause the flood of tears

Rejection held a lesson
Of how bad people can be
Rejection was your confession
That you never wanted me

I needed you to hurt me
Because you only loved yourself
I needed you break me
Because I needed to heal myself

The pain was my motivation
To be the person I dreamed to be
The pain was my motivation
To find my happiness and peace

I needed you to hurt me
For me to know I deserved more
I needed you to break me
For me to finally walk out the door

Losing you was a blessing
It freed me from your pain
Losing you was a gift
It allowed me to start again

I needed you to hurt me
Or I would never have met him
I needed you to break me
So I could let real love in

Second Choice

I never liked second place
But I always followed the rules
What you did was a disgrace
And made me feel like a fool

On one hand, I want to know why
On the other, I want to start running
How could you be that guy
How could you be so cunning

You said you cared about me
Was that ever true?
You said I had your heart
But did I ever have you?

I don't care where you go
I don't care what you have to say
It's too late for an apology
I just want you to go away

I won't let you keep hurting me
I have found my voice
I have too much self-respect
I won't be your second choice

Runaway

I sometimes wish to runaway
And leave this world behind
But I cannot leave the ones I love
Running away would be unkind
So I stay, despite the pain
And make it through another day
But I feel it is a constant battle
To stay and pretend to be okay

Lost

I can't seem to find it
It's nowhere to be seen
And there's no hints or clues
Of who I'm meant to be
I'm left to solve the puzzle
Without a reference guide
When what I really want to do
Is runaway and hide
Perhaps I need a map to know
What bridge needs to be crossed
But what good is a map in darkness?
Right now I just feel lost

Books

Books have always been my home
The place where I feel safe
The inked pages my eyes would roam
And there was my escape

When I was sad, I would find a book
And read until I felt okay
The stories would give me a new outlook
And help improve my day

But sometimes the monsters appear
And make the world all dark
One monster with his evil sneer
Stole my reading spark

For a time, I couldn't find my joy
Feeling broken and lost
Like a child missing their favourite toy
I wanted it back at any cost

It took a massive change to find it
It took him to be gone
The person who always discouraged it
Who was clearly a moron

Once I escaped from his toxic crew
I finally felt free
Through many book's pages I flew
To find the new me

I still love my books and reading
That remains the same
But this me is stronger and fighting
To never lose my flame

Don't let anyone take your spark
Or steal away a dream
Hold onto your light in the dark
And be your own sunbeam

Mum

You gave my life
You paved the way
For me to become
Who I am today

You healed me when I was wounded
Picked me up each time I fell
Encouraged every idea and dream
And supported me to do well

No relationship is perfect
We do sometime fight
But even on our darkest days
You are my source of light

I am so lucky to have you
Much luckier than some
But this is all just to say
Thank you for being my mum

Magic

When people think of magic
They think magicians and tricks
But the truth about real magic
Is it's what makes us all tick

Magic is the air surrounding you
Invisible but filling up our lungs
Carrying sweet smells with the breeze
And the words from our tongues

Magic is the earth below us
The foundation of our lives
Providing us a place to sleep, play
And the food we need to survive

Magic is the water supporting us
Rushing through rivers and falling from the sky
It's in our bodies and on the earth
Without it we would die

Magic is the flame warming us
It's there to keep us warm
It will also light our way
And protect us from the storm

Magic is in the moments
A smile, a tear, a laugh
It can heal wounds, new and old
And set us on our path

Magic is within us all
In kind words and compassion
And that's the kind of magic
That should always be in fashion

Home

Home is not a place
It's not a location
It's not a building
It's not a house

A house does not make a home

Home is a feeling
It's feeling comfortable
It's feeling safe
It's feeling loved

Love is what makes a home

Dad

You left me alone
When I needed you most
You put me through hell
Because you were lost
Why do you blame me?
Why are you so mad?
You wanted to kill yourself
Was I really that bad?
Tell me what did I do
To deserve your painful blow
But at the end of the day
I already know
I never was your princess
I never was your world
You didn't want a daughter
You didn't want a girl
I survived your disapproval
I learned to live without your love
But deep within my soul
I feel I was never good enough
I learned not to miss you
I learned not to be sad
But what really hurt me most is
All I wanted was a dad

Work

It was supposed to be my start
A place I went for money
But what happened to me there
Was anything fun funny
I was dismissed as too young
And treated like a fool
Blamed for every mistake
In ways that felt so cruel

It started with my performance
And how I seemed to struggle
But I had replaced three people
And had all their work to juggle
Then it was my appearance
And the type of food I eat
Saying if I ate more salads
I could be more petite

I became more anxious
Had regular panic attacks
I dreaded going to work
Because no one had my back
The comments about my weight
Led to an eating disorder
Every day was a physically struggle

Workdays became full torture

No matter how hard I tried
The bullying never stopped
It took a scary wakeup call
Where my body simply dropped
I sent in my notice
I used up all my leave
I got myself away
From the people killing me

No job outranks your mental health
No bullying is worth the paycheck
You should not be feeling helpless
You should not be a nervous wreck
Although it's tough to say goodbye
To financial stability
It is so much nicer living life
Without their hostility

November

I will always remember the fifth of November
The day you took my breath away
And though at the time you could not have
realised
You saved my life that day

Soft golden hair, a cheeky smile
And the bluest of blue eyes
A little boy born early
but ready for the fight

Each day you faced your battles
Some days you made us cry
But you were born with determination
And it encouraged me to try

I started my own tough journey
One you would observe
The challenges I would face
To be the big sister you deserve

I had to learn to heal my heart
And learn to live with scars
But you taught me to dream beyond that
And shoot for the stars

I will always remember the fifth of November
The day you came to be
And although you do not realise yet
Thank you for saving me

Dream

When I dream about the future
I am intrigued by what I see
If what I dream is to be true
It's not a standard fairytale for me
Though this is not a bad thing
No cause for any sorrow
Because if this is to be my future
I'll look forward to tomorrow

My dream shows me peaceful
Settled in a cosy house
A place filled with joy and laughter
And a kind, supportive spouse
There may or may not be children
Or a fur baby or three
But there's a beautiful fireplace
And a room I call my library

The walls are filled with puzzles
Put together over the years
Our artwork shows off who we are
And displays our fun souvenirs
The yard is filled with flowers
Veggie gardens and fruit trees
Maybe there will also be chickens

And a hive for our own bees

The best part about this dream
Is it may one day come true
Because I get to share this dream
As it is a dream shared by you
And when the dream inevitably ends
I have no reason to feel blue
Because I wake up in the arms
Of my dream man, you

Impossible

I dream of the impossible
Knowing it may never happen
But the whisper in my heart
Keeps my mind imagining

For anything can be possible
With magic in your soul
and hope flowing through my veins
Making me feel whole

And so I light a candle or two
And ask for what I dream
Even though it's not immediate
The magic I have seen

It really is incredible
The things I can achieve
For the impossible is possible
If only you believe

Beach

The beach is my safe space
A place I can be me
The beach is my safe space
A place my soul feels free

I can scream, I can cry
I can curse up to the sky

I can walk, I can swim
I don't need a gym

I can laugh, I can dance
I can have a great romance

I can breathe, I can think
I don't need to sink

The beach is my safe space
A place I can be me
The beach is my safe space
A place my soul feels free

Mr Read

I met you on a cool winter's day
And what a day that was
The rush, the excitement, the moments
I wish I could hit pause

Coffee, gnocchi and a walk in the park
Was the only just the start
But I knew by the end of that day
You would have my heart

Weeks of lockdowns then weeks of fun
Getting to know you was a dream
You match my weird, support my passions
And helped repair my self-esteem

Then one day the darkness hit
I was haunted by my past
I didn't feel I deserved your love
And thought it wouldn't last

I feared my darkness had scared you away
And you wouldn't want me anymore
That you would think I was 'too hard, too much'
As others had said before

Instead, you pulled me closer
And told me it was all okay
You assured me I was safe and loved
And you wouldn't run away

Not only do you heal my wounds
You read me like a book
I feel loved, supported, respected
And seen with every look

You are always there when I need a hug
Be it night or daylight hours
And you always know how to make me smile
Like it's one of your superpowers

I never thought a man like you existed
Or that you would even want to be mine
Who would have known I'd fall in love
With a man whose name is my pastime